JOHANN PACHELBEL

Canon

D major / D-Dur

Arranged for Piano by / Bearbeitung für Klavier von

Mary Cohen

ALLE RECHTE VORBEHALTEN · ALL RIGHTS RESERVED

EDITION PETERS

LEIPZIG · LONDON · NEW YORK

PREFACE

When 24-year-old Johann Pachelbel arrived in Eisenach in 1677 he was befriended by 'Town Musician' Ambrosius Bach (who eight years later would have a son called Johann Sebastian). Although Pachelbel left Eisenach in 1678 to take up a post as organist in Erfurt, his friendship with the Bach family continued. Ambrosius sent him his son, Johann Christoph, to continue his musical education; then in 1680 he registered Pachelbel as godfather to his daughter Johanna Juditha.

As an organist (and an expert in the mechanics and maintenance of organs), Pachelbel was highly respected; over the next 28 years he held posts in Stuttgart, Gotha, and finally Nuremberg (the town of his birth). He must also have been a good teacher, for his pupil Johann Christoph Bach took over from him in Erfurt and remained there until 1721.

As a composer Johann Pachelbel wrote mainly for keyboard instruments, but from time to time he produced chamber music for strings and basso continuo. Sadly, most of the manuscripts for these chamber works have been lost. However, one particular piece is mentioned in a letter, written by the music director of Eisenach: he says that, at a wedding in October 1694, likely that of Johann Christoph Bach, three fine musicians (Johann Veit Hoffmann, Ambrosius Bach and Johann Pachelbel) were all 'vying with each other on the violin'. The exuberant piece they were performing may well have been the famous and much-loved Canon in D.

Mary Cohen

VORWORT

Als der 24-jährige Johann Pachelbel 1677 nach Eisenach kam, freundete er sich mit dem Stadtmusikus Ambrosius Bach an (der acht Jahre später Vater eines Sohnes namens Johann Sebastian werden sollte). Obwohl Pachelbel 1678 als Organist nach Erfurt wechselte, blieb die Freundschaft zur Familie Bach bestehen. Ambrosius schickte ihm seinen Sohn Johann Christoph zur Ausbildung, und 1680 ließ er Pachelbel als Paten seiner Tochter Johanna Juditha eintragen.

Pachelbel genoss als Organist (wie auch als Fachmann für die Funktion und Reparatur von Orgeln) hohes Ansehen; in den folgenden 28 Jahren war er in Stuttgart, Gotha und zuletzt in seiner Heimatstadt Nürnberg tätig. Zudem muss er ein guter Lehrer gewesen sein, denn sein Schüler Johann Christoph Bach wurde in Erfurt sein Nachfolger und blieb dort bis 1721.

Als Komponist schrieb Johann Pachelbel vorwiegend für Tasteninstrumente, schuf gelegentlich aber auch Kammermusik für Streicher und Continuo. Leider sind die meisten Handschriften dieser Ensemblewerke nicht erhalten, doch wird eines der Stücke in einem Brief des Eisenacher Stadtkantors vom Oktober 1694 erwähnt: Er berichtet, dass bei einer Hochzeit – vermutlich der von Johann Christoph Bach – „Sie dreie [Johann Veit Hoffmann, Ambrosius Bach und Johann Pachelbel] mit einander in der Violine certireten". Das überschwängliche Stück, in dem die drei erfahrenen Musiker miteinander wetteiferten, war womöglich der bekannte und beliebte Kanon D-Dur.

Mary Cohen
Übersetzung: Arne Muus

Canon

D major / D-Dur

Johann Pachelbel (1653–1706)
Arranged by Mary Cohen

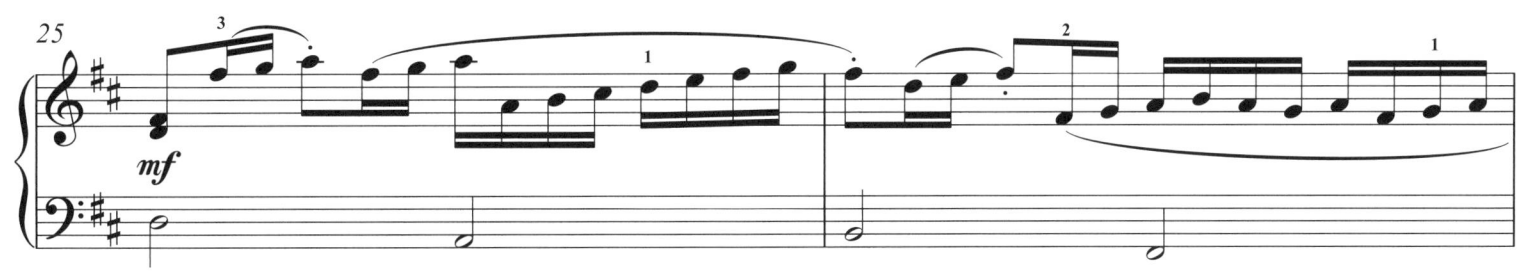
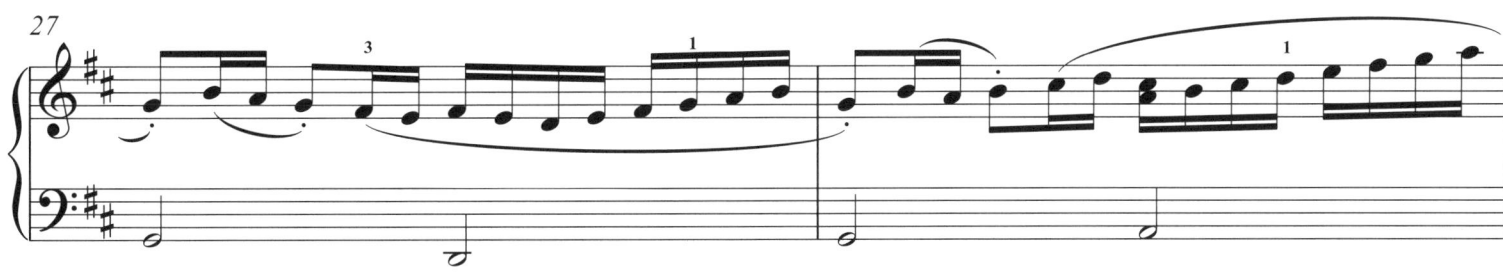